EDGE BOOKS™

NASCAR RACING

The Daytona 500

By A. R. Schaefer

Consultant:
Betty L. Carlan
Research Librarian
International Motorsports Hall of Fame
Talladega, Alabama

Capstone
press

Mankato, Minnesota

Edge Books are published by Capstone Press
151 Good Counsel Drive, P.O. Box 669, Mankato, Minnesota 56002
www.capstonepress.com

Library of Congress Cataloging-in-Publication Data
Schaefer, A. R. (Adam Richard), 1976–
    The Daytona 500 / by A. R. Schaefer.
    p. cm.—(Edge Books NASCAR racing)
    Summary: Discusses the history and design of Daytona International Speedway
along with the Daytona 500's most exciting finishes and famous racers.
    Includes bibliographical references and index.
    ISBN 0-7368-2423-5 (hardcover)
    1. Daytona 500 (Automobile race)—Juvenile literature. [1. Daytona 500
(Automobile race) 2. Stock car racing.] I. Title. II. Series.
GV1033.5.D39S4 2004
796.72'06'875921—dc22   2003012712

Editorial Credits
Tom Adamson, editor; Jason Knudson, designer; Jo Miller, photo researcher

Photo Credits
AP/Wide World Photos/Glenn Smith, 6; Terry Renna, 5
Artemis Images, cover (racecar)
Corbis/Bettmann, 17
Florida State Archives, 13
Getty Images/Jon Ferrey, 29
SportsChrome-USA, cover (background), 7; Brian Spurlock, 28; Evan Pinkus, 23;
    Greg Crisp, 15, 19; Scott Cunningham, 25
Sports Gallery Inc./Dick Conway, 18, 26, 27; Joe Robbins, 9, 10, 11

1 2 3 4 5 6 09 08 07 06 05 04

Table of Contents

CHAPTER 1

Jeff Gordon's Move

On February 14, 1999, NASCAR fans enjoyed one of the most exciting and closest Daytona 500s ever. Rusty Wallace led most of the race. Jeff Gordon, who started on the pole, stayed in the top 10 for most of the race. Dale Earnhardt also fought with the leaders.

The battle for first place heated up at the end. Gordon made some risky passes in the final 20 laps. With 13 laps to go, Earnhardt was just ahead of Gordon. Gordon went around him into second place. Three laps later, Gordon went below Wallace on the frontstretch and took the lead. Gordon had to cut in front of Wallace to avoid hitting the back of a lapped car. This move sent Wallace to an eighth-place finish.

Gordon (#24) passed Wallace (#2) and squeezed him out of first place.

Learn about:

→ A risky pass

→ A last lap duel

→ The Great American Race

Gordon crossed the finish line just ahead of Earnhardt.

The race was not over yet. Earnhardt passed Wallace to get behind Gordon with just a few laps to go. Earnhardt caught Gordon on the last lap and rode his bumper most of the way. Earnhardt took a run at Gordon on the backstretch, but Gordon held him off. Earnhardt looked for room one more time as they came down the frontstretch to the finish line. There was no room. Gordon crossed the finish line 0.128 second ahead of Earnhardt.

> "Trying to keep [Earnhardt] behind me is one of the hardest things I've ever done at Daytona."
>
> —Jeff Gordon, sportsillustrated.cnn.com, 2-26-99

The Daytona 500

The Daytona 500 is the biggest NASCAR race of the year. It has been nicknamed "The Great American Race." Many drivers call it their Super Bowl. The race takes place each February at Daytona International Speedway in Daytona Beach, Florida. The Daytona 500 always opens the NASCAR season.

Gordon celebrated after winning his second Daytona 500.

CHAPTER 2

Daytona International Speedway

Daytona International Speedway is best known for hosting the Daytona 500. Its design and history make it one of the most famous racetracks in the world.

Design

Daytona is a tri-oval. The tri-oval has three legs. The backstretch is one leg, and the frontstretch is made up of two legs.

The track is 2.5 miles (4 kilometers) long and 40 feet (12 meters) wide. Drivers race 200 laps to complete the 500-mile (805-kilometer) race. The backstretch is the longest leg of the track. This flat stretch is 3,000 feet (914 meters) long. The frontstretch is made up of two smaller legs. They are each 1,900 feet (579 meters) long. These legs meet at the start-finish line.

The banked frontstretch helps make Daytona a fast track.

Learn about:

→ **Track banking**

→ **Drafting**

→ **Beach-Road course**

The high-banked turns at Daytona allow cars to maintain high speeds.

The banked turns at Daytona help cars take corners at high speeds. The small turn at the start-finish line is banked 18 degrees. The other turns are banked 31 degrees. Cars can build up great speed on the long backstretch and steep banks.

Restrictor Plates

When Winston Cup cars race at Daytona, they must use restrictor plates. The plates keep the cars from going more than about 190 miles (300 kilometers) an hour. Drivers can keep better control of their cars under this speed. Without the plates, the cars could go about 230 miles (370 kilometers) an hour. This speed is unsafe for drivers, crew members, and fans.

With the restrictor plates, the only way to gain extra speed in the Daytona 500 is by drafting. Drivers get close to the car in front of theirs, almost touching it. Cars have less air resistance this close to the car. They then use the draft as a slingshot to pass the car on a turn.

In the Daytona 500, drivers draft to gain extra speed.

History

In 1947, Bill France started NASCAR in Daytona Beach. His idea was for NASCAR to hold several series of races every year. The drivers who did the best over the year would win a championship. The Daytona 500 became an important race because it took place where NASCAR began.

Few early racetracks were good for racing. Most races were held on dirt tracks. The track at Daytona Beach was called the Beach-Road course. The 4-mile (6.4-kilometer) track was half on a beach and half on a highway. The heavy cars made deep ruts in the sand.

France saw a chance to do something different. More NASCAR races were being run on paved tracks. The track on the beach needed to be replaced. France decided to build a huge racetrack.

The new racetrack was designed with the fans in mind. Daytona's big tri-oval gave fans good sight lines. They could see what was happening on the opposite leg. The track was finished in time for the first Daytona 500 in 1959.

The Beach-Road course was replaced by Daytona International Speedway.

TRACK DIAGRAM
Daytona International Speedway

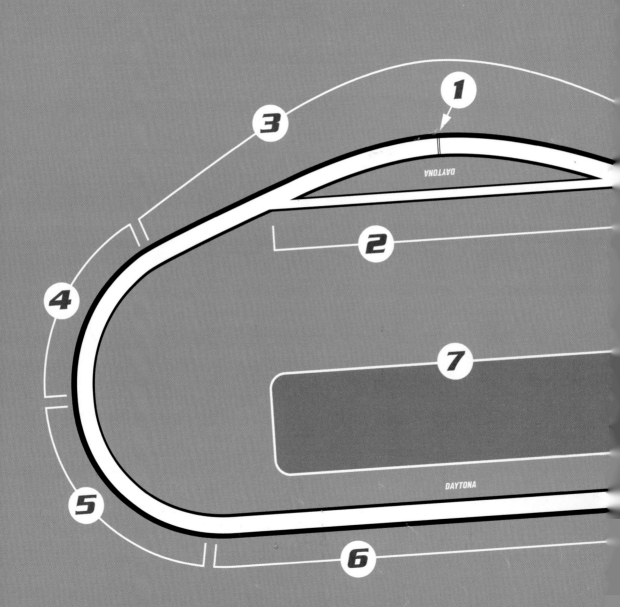

CHAPTER 3

Famous Races

Daytona holds two major NASCAR races every year. The Daytona 500 is always held in February. The Pepsi 400 is later in the year. The Daytona 500 has had many famous finishes.

Incredible Finish

The 1976 race was one of the most exciting in history. With 13 laps to go, Richard Petty took the lead. David Pearson was right behind him. Petty and Pearson were rivals during the 1970s. They finished first and second more than 60 times during their careers.

On the last lap, Pearson drove his car right behind Petty's. On the backstretch, Pearson sped up and passed Petty as they entered the turn. Pearson's speed made his car go high into the turn. Petty drove low, just to the left of Pearson. As Pearson came down, the cars collided. Both cars hit the wall and spun into the infield grass.

Petty and Pearson crashed on the last lap of the 1976 race.

Learn about:

→ **Last lap crash**
→ **Richard Petty**
→ **Photo finish**

17

The two cars stopped. Pearson then drove his car back on the track toward the finish line. Petty could not get his car started again. Pearson crossed the finish line going 20 miles (32 kilometers) an hour to win the race.

No one has won more Daytona 500s than Richard Petty.

Richard Petty

Richard Petty is known as one of the best NASCAR drivers ever. He won the NASCAR championship seven times. He also won the Daytona 500 a record seven times.

Petty was named Rookie of the Year in 1959. He won his first Daytona 500 and his first NASCAR championship in 1964. He won his second 500 two years later. He was the dominant racer at Daytona in the 1970s. He won in 1971, 1973, 1974, and 1979. Petty won his last Daytona 500 in 1981.

Petty won 200 races during his 34 years in NASCAR's top racing division. He retired in 1992. The Petty family has a long history of success at Daytona. Petty's father, Lee, won the first Daytona 500 in 1959. Lee Petty died in 2000 at age 86. Richard's son Kyle won the pole at Daytona in 1993.

The First Race

The first Daytona 500 was held February 22, 1959. The drivers had never before raced on a track like Daytona. The new pavement, high-banked turns, and long track meant drivers could go faster than on most other racetracks.

The first 500 had a close finish. Johnny Beauchamp's and Lee Petty's cars crossed the finish line at almost exactly the same time.

Race officials were not sure who won. They gave the trophy to Beauchamp and called him the unofficial winner. The officials studied film and pictures of the finish for three days. They finally declared that Petty had won the race and gave the trophy to Petty.

"We won't be caught off guard again. We'll install a photo finish camera at the line."
—Bill France, NASCAR Greatest Races

The Daytona 500
Race Statistics

Year	Driver	Car	Starting Position	Prize Money
1959	Lee Petty	Oldsmobile	15	$19,050
1960	Junior Johnson	Chevrolet	9	$19,600
1961	Marvin Panch	Pontiac	4	$21,050
1962	Fireball Roberts	Pontiac	1	$24,190
1963	Tiny Lund	Ford	12	$24,550
1964	Richard Petty	Plymouth	2	$33,300
1965	Fred Lorenzen	Ford	4	$27,100
1966	Richard Petty	Plymouth	1	$28,150
1967	Mario Andretti	Ford	12	$48,900
1968	Cale Yarborough	Mercury	1	$47,250
1969	LeeRoy Yarbrough	Ford	19	$38,950
1970	Pete Hamilton	Plymouth	9	$44,850
1971	Richard Petty	Plymouth	5	$45,450
1972	A. J. Foyt	Mercury	2	$44,600
1973	Richard Petty	Dodge	7	$36,100
1974	Richard Petty	Dodge	2	$39,650
1975	Benny Parsons	Chevrolet	32	$43,905
1976	David Pearson	Mercury	7	$46,800
1977	Cale Yarborough	Chevrolet	4	$63,700
1978	Bobby Allison	Ford	33	$56,300
1979	Richard Petty	Oldsmobile	13	$73,900
1980	Buddy Baker	Oldsmobile	1	$102,175
1981	Richard Petty	Buick	8	$90,575
1982	Bobby Allison	Buick	7	$120,630
1983	Cale Yarborough	Pontiac	8	$119,600
1984	Cale Yarborough	Chevrolet	1	$160,300
1985	Bill Elliott	Ford	1	$185,500
1986	Geoffrey Bodine	Chevrolet	2	$192,715
1987	Bill Elliott	Ford	1	$204,150
1988	Bobby Allison	Buick	3	$202,940
1989	Darrell Waltrip	Chevrolet	2	$184,900
1990	Derrike Cope	Chevrolet	12	$188,150
1991	Ernie Irvan	Chevrolet	2	$233,000
1992	Davey Allison	Ford	6	$244,050
1993	Dale Jarrett	Chevrolet	2	$238,200
1994	Sterling Marlin	Chevrolet	4	$258,275
1995	Sterling Marlin	Chevrolet	3	$300,460
1996	Dale Jarrett	Ford	7	$360,775
1997	Jeff Gordon	Chevrolet	6	$377,410
1998	Dale Earnhardt	Chevrolet	4	$1,059,805
1999	Jeff Gordon	Chevrolet	1	$1,172,246
2000	Dale Jarrett	Ford	1	$1,277,975
2001	Michael Waltrip	Chevrolet	19	$1,331,185
2002	Ward Burton	Dodge	19	$1,409,017
2003	Michael Waltrip	Chevrolet	4	$1,419,406

CHAPTER 4

Famous Racers

All of the great NASCAR drivers have raced at Daytona. Richard Petty holds the record for most Daytona 500 wins. He has won seven 500s. Other drivers have also had success in the Daytona 500.

Dale Earnhardt

Dale Earnhardt was one of the most famous NASCAR drivers of all time. In 1979, he was the NASCAR Rookie of the Year. In 1980, he won the series championship. He won the series championship seven times in 15 years. He won 76 NASCAR races during his career. Many people consider him the best driver ever.

Some people called Earnhardt the "Intimidator."

Learn about:

→ Dale Earnhardt

→ Cale Yarborough

→ Dale Jarrett

For most of his career, Earnhardt could not win the Daytona 500. He won every other major race. But he always seemed to have bad luck at Daytona. Finally, on his 21st try, he won. He was 46 years old when he won in 1998.

Three years later, on the last lap of the 500, Earnhardt was in third place coming around Turn 3. He lost control of his car and started spinning. The car went to the bottom of the bank and hit a flat spot. The flat spot sent his car flying to the top of the track and into the wall. Earnhardt died instantly in the collision.

"This win is for all our fans and all the people who told me, 'Dale, this is your year,' . . . The Daytona 500 is over. And we won it! We won it!"

—Dale Earnhardt, www.daleearnhardt.net, 2-15-98

Earnhardt finally won the Daytona 500 in 1998 after coming close many times.

Cale Yarborough

Only four NASCAR drivers have won more races than Cale Yarborough has. Yarborough won his first race in 1965 in Valdosta, Georgia. He won 83 Winston Cup races during his career.

Yarborough now owns a racing school in Florida.

Yarborough won his last Daytona 500 in 1984.

Yarborough is a four-time winner of the Daytona 500. He won the 500 in 1968, 1977, 1983, and 1984. He has also started on the pole position four times.

Yarborough dominated NASCAR for three straight years from 1976 to 1978. He is the only NASCAR driver in history to win the series championship three years in a row. In 1976, he won four races in a row.

Jarrett was one of the best racers during the 1990s.

Dale Jarrett

Dale Jarrett has won the Daytona 500 three times. Jarrett won the race in 1993, 1996, and 2000. He has won more than 30 Winston Cup races.

Jarrett was good at sports when he was in high school. He was offered a scholarship to play golf in college. He turned down the scholarship and started working at his father's racetrack. He then tried driving in a race. He was hooked.

Jarrett started driving in the Winston Cup Series in 1984. He drove in the series for seven years before he won his first race in 1991. In 1993, he won his first Daytona 500 and became a star.

The Great American Race

The Daytona 500 kicks off the NASCAR season every February. "The Great American Race" is where stock car legends are made. Daytona's high banks and controlled speeds give fans an exciting race every year.

Jarrett won his third Daytona 500 in 2000.

Glossary

backstretch (BAK-strech)—the straight part of a racetrack that is opposite the frontstretch

bank (BANGK)—the angle of the track; if a track has a high bank, the top of the track is much higher than the bottom of the track.

drafting (DRAF-ting)—a strategy in which a driver closely follows another car to reduce air resistance

frontstretch (FRUHNT-strech)—the straight part of a racetrack where the race begins and ends

infield (IN-feeld)—the area inside a racetrack, surrounded on all sides by the track

pole (POHL)—the inside spot at the front of the line at the beginning of a race

restrictor plate (ri-STRIKT-ur PLAYT)— a device that limits the power of a racecar's engine; the restrictor plate keeps down the car's speed for safety.

rookie (RUK-ee)—a first-year driver

series (SIHR-eez)—a group of races that make up one season; drivers earn points for finishing races in a series.

Read More

Barber, Phil. *Stock Car's Greatest Race: The First and the Fastest.* The World of NASCAR. Excelsior, Minn.: Tradition Publishing, 2003.

Johnstone, Michael. *NASCAR.* The Need for Speed. Minneapolis: LernerSports, 2002.

Stewart, Mark. *The Daytona 500.* The Watts History of Sports. New York: Franklin Watts, 2002.

Useful Addresses

Daytona International Speedway
1801 West International Speedway Boulevard
Daytona Beach, FL 32114

International Motorsports Hall of Fame
P.O. Box 1018
Talladega, AL 35161

NASCAR
P.O. Box 2875
Daytona Beach, FL 32120

Richard Petty Museum
142 West Academy Street
Randleman, NC 27317

Internet Sites

FactHound offers a safe, fun way to find Internet sites related to this book. All of the sites on FactHound have been researched by our staff.

Here's how:

1. Visit *www.facthound.com*
2. Type in this special code **0736824235** for age-appropriate sites. Or enter a search word related to this book for a more general search.
3. Click on the **Fetch It** button.

FactHound will fetch the best sites for you!

Index